ISOBEL Y. FISHER & ROBERT J. DIXSON

BEGINNING LESSONS IN ENGLISH

A NEW REVISED EDITION

A

Regents Publishing Company, Inc.

Cover design: Paul Gamarello
Text design: Suzanne Bennett & Associates
Illustrations: Iris Van Rhynbach

ISBN 0-88345-530-7

Published by Regents Publishing Company, Inc.
2 Park Avenue
New York, New York 10016
Printed in the United States of America

10 9 8 7 6 5 4 3 2

FOREWORD

Beginning Lessons in English offers a direct and effective method of learning English. It emphasizes the spoken language and focuses attention on pronunciation and conversation. There is a minimum of formal explanation. Instead, each lesson introduces new items of grammar by pattern practice, with constant reinforcement in succeeding lessons.

This 1983 revision has been expanded and updated. *Beginning Lessons in English Book A* has a companion volume in *Book B* and both are followed by *Second Book in English*. The three books are carefully sequenced to provide a challenging, yet precisely-metered course in English as a second language to students in a variety of English-learning settings.

The texts are designed to be adaptable to a wide variety of teaching techniques. We suggest, however, that the teacher start each period with a review of the previous session's work before beginning a new lesson. Because the text introduces new grammar and new speech patterns at a steady rate, no more than one lesson should be covered in any session. The class should maintain a schedule of constant review and repetition, and should not proceed to a new lesson until students have first demonstrated oral mastery of the current lesson.

Teachers should encourage students to learn full-form (complete sentence) patterns but also to learn and practice the more common, contracted-form patterns for use in their conversational English.

As a homework supplement, the teacher might want to consider the appropriate level of *Regents English Workbook*. The three volumes are also of graded difficulty and offer helpful additional practice on target structures. Such supplementary texts as *Pronunciation Exercises in English* and a three-level reading series are also available within the Dixson English Series from Regents Publishing Company.

CONTENTS

1. Introductory Vocabulary   1

2. Introductory Vocabulary   3

3. PresentTense *to be,* statements and questions;
Days of the week   6

4. Possessive Adjectives; Numbers; *There is, there are*   10

5. Present Tense *to need, to want, to have;* Plurals   14

6. Third Person; Present Tense negative *to be*   18

7. Present Continuous Tense; Time   21

8. Past Tense *to be;* Past Continuous Tense; Opposites   25

9. Short Answers affirmative and negative *to be*   29

10. Past Tense regular and irregular verbs; Opposites   33

11. Personal Pronouns, Objective Case   37

12. Articles *a, an;* Prepositions   41

13. Present Tense questions, *do, does;* Ordinal Numbers;
Days of the week   45

14. Present Tense negatives *don't, doesn't;*
Months of the year   49

15. Past Tense; Opposites; Seasons of the year   53

16. Past Tense questions; Colors; Opposites   58

17. Past Tense negatives *didn't;* Past Tense Short Answers
affirmative and negative   61

18. Past Tense; Adjectives; Opposites   65

19. Future Tense *to be;* Numbers; Money   69

20. Future Tense; Prepositions   73

21. Future Tense negative and Future Tense Short Answers
    affirmative and negative   76

22. Review   79

23. *This, that, these, those;* Review   82

24. Comparatives; Review   86

25. Past Tense; Tenses Review   90

26. Review of Present and Past *to be*   95

27. Review of Future *to be* and Opposites   100

28. Review of Tenses (time expressions), Personal Pronouns,
    and *there is, there are*   104

29. Review of *there* and Plurals   109

30. Review of Third Person and of Tenses
    and Personal Pronouns   113

31. Review of Possessive Adjectives, Time, Short Answers,
    and Colors   131

BEGINNING LESSONS IN
ENGLISH
A

LESSON 1

What is your name?   My name is _____.
What's* your name?   My name's* _____.
What's her name?   Her name's _____.
What's his name?   His name's _____.

What is this?      This is a pencil.
What's this?   This is a pencil.

What's this?   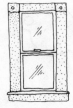   This is a book.

What's this?      This is a window.

What's this?   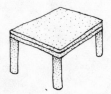   This is a table.

What's this?   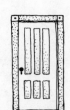   This is a door.

* When we speak, we usually use the contraction *'s* for the word *is*. The *'s* is attached to the preceding word.

What's this? 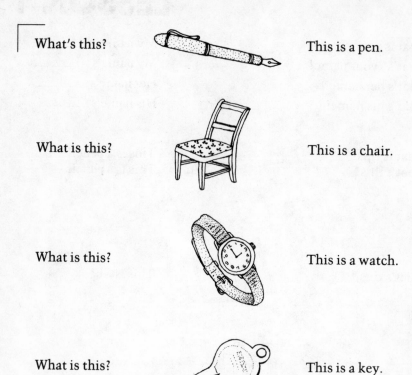 This is a pen.

What is this? This is a chair.

What is this? This is a watch.

What is this? This is a key.

LESSON 2

What is this?
What's this?

It is a hat.
It's* a hat.

What's this?

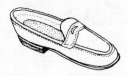

It's a shoe.

What's this?

It's a glove.

What's this?

It's a sweater.

What's this?

It's a shirt.

What's this?

It's a glass.

* When we speak, we usually use the contraction *it's* for *it is.*

What's this?  It's a cup.

What's this?  It's a dog.

What's this?  It's a cat.

Is this a hat
or a book?  It is a book.
It's a book.

Is this a table
or a glove?  It's _____.

Is this a shirt
or a door?  It's _____.

Is this a pen
or a pencil?

 It's _____.

Is this a chair
or a window?

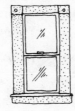 It's _____.

Is this a cup
or a glass?

 It's _____.

Is this a cat
or a dog?

 It's _____.

LESSON 3

I GRAMMAR

Present Tense *to be*

Full Form	*Contraction**	*Full Form*	*Contraction*
I am	I'm	we are	we're
you are	you're	you are	you're
he is	he's ⎫		
she is	she's ⎬	they are	they're
it is	it's ⎭		

II PRACTICAL INFORMATION

The Days of the Week

Sunday	**Wednesday**
Monday	**Thursday**
Tuesday	**Friday**
Saturday	

What day is today?

Today is _____.

III PRACTICE DRILL

I am a teacher.	I'm a teacher.
You are a student.	You're a student.
He is a student.	He's a student.
She is a student.	She's a student.
We are students.	We're students.
John and Mary are students.	They're students.

IV EXERCISES

A. Fill in the blanks.

1. I _____ a teacher.
   (I __am__ a teacher.)

2. You _____ a student.

3. This _____ a book.

4. She _____ a student.

---

* When we speak, we generally use the contractions *I'm, you're,* etc.

5. John and Mary _____ students.

6. They _____ students.

7. He _____ a teacher.

8. Miss Fields _____ a woman.

9. She _____ a French teacher.

10. She _____ a good teacher.

11. We _____ students.

12. Mr. Jones _____ a man.

13. He _____ a mathematics teacher.

14. He _____ a good teacher.

B. Repeat Exercise A using contractions.

Example: 1. I _____ **a teacher.**
   (I'm a teacher.)

C. Substitute the words in the sentence "I am a student."

Example: I am a student.
   He
   He is a student.
   They
   They are students.

1. Mary
2. You
3. They
4. Charles and Diana
5. We

6. You
7. I
8. He
9. She
10. Miss Taylor

D. Repeat Exercise C using contractions.

Example: I'm a student.
   He
   He's a student.
   They
   They're students.

E. Answer these questions.

1. Is Maria a man or a woman?
   (She's a woman.)
2. Are you a teacher or a student?
3. Is John a woman?
4. Is Ellen a teacher?
5. Am I a teacher?
6. Is he a teacher?
7. Is he a student?
8. Are you a man or a woman?
9. Is this a book?
10. Are Charles and Diana students?
11. Are you students?
12. Is Mrs. Ryan a woman?
13. Is this a door or a window?
14. Are you teachers?
15. Is Mr. James a man?

V CONVERSATION

I open the door.

I walk into the room.

I close the door.

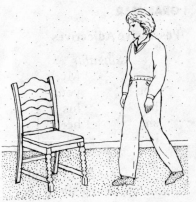

I walk to my chair.

I sit down.

I read my book.
I study my lesson.

LESSON 4

I GRAMMAR

Possessive Adjectives

	Singular		*Plural*
I	My	we	our
you	your	you	your
he	his		
she	her	they	their
it	its		

> *I* walk to *my* chair.
> *You* walk to *your* chair.
> *He* walks to *his* chair.
> *She* walks to *her* chair.
> *We* walk to *our* chairs.
> *They* walk to *their* chairs.

II PRACTICAL INFORMATION

Numbers

1 one	6 six
2 two	7 seven
3 three	8 eight
4 four	9 nine
5 five	10 ten

III PRACTICE DRILL

A. I open the door.
    I walk into the room.
    I close the door.
    I walk to my chair.
    I sit down.
    I read my book.
    I study my lesson.

B. Repeat the Practice Drill, but change *I* to *you.*
    (*You* open the door.)

IV EXERCISES

A. Fill in the blanks with the correct Possessive Adjective.

1. I walk to _____ chair.
    (I walk to my chair.)

2. You walk to _____ chair.

3. She walks to _____ chair.

4. He walks to _____ chair.

5. *Ms. Evans walks to _____ chair.

6. Albert walks to _____ chair.

7. The woman walks to _____ chair.

8. They walk to _____ chair.

9. We walk to _____ chair.

10. The boy walks to _____ chair.

11. Mr. Roberts walks to _____ chair.

B. Fill in the blanks with the words for the numbers.

1. _____*one*_____   6. _____

2. _____   7. _____

3. _____   8. _____

4. _____   9. _____

5. _____   10. _____

---

* *Ms.* is a courtesy title for a woman. *Mr.* is the title for a man. *Miss* is the courtesy title for an unmarried woman. *Mrs.* is the title for a married woman.

V CONVERSATION

There is—There are

This *is* a picture of a room.
There is one table in this room.
There is one window in this room.
There are two pictures on the wall.
There is a rug on the floor.
There are three chairs in this room.
There are curtains on the window.
Is there a table in the room?
Yes, *there is. There is* one table in the room.
Are there flowers in the room?
Yes, *there are. There are* flowers by the window.

A. Answer these questions.

1. Is there a rug on the floor?
    (Yes, <u>there is</u>. <u>There is</u> one rug on the floor.)

2. Is there a table in this room?

3. Are there two chairs or three chairs in this room?

4. Is there a window in the room?

5. Are there flowers in this room?

6. Are there two pictures or three pictures on the wall?

7. Is there a door in this room?

8. Are there curtains on the window?

9. Are there pictures on the wall of your classroom?

10. Is there a blackboard on the wall of your classroom?

11. How many windows are there in your classroom?

12. How many doors are there in your classroom?

B. Ask questions about the picture or about your classroom.

LESSON 5

I GRAMMAR

A. Present Tense *to need, to want, to have*

I need a book.
I want a pen.
I have a pencil.

You need a book.
You want a pen.
You have a pencil.

We need a book.
We want a pen.
We have a pencil.

They need a book.
They want a pen.
They have a pencil.

B. Plural Form

one hand —two hands
one thumb —three thumbs
one picture —four pictures
one chair —five chairs
one boy —six boys
one girl —seven girls

one table —eight tables
one finger —nine fingers
one man —ten men
one woman —eleven women
one child —twelve children
one foot —thirteen feet

II PRACTICE DRILL

We walk into the room.
We walk to our chairs.
We sit down.
We pick up our pencils.
We write our names.

III EXERCISES

A. Substitute the words in the sentence "I need a book."

> **Example: I need a book.**
> *You*
> You need a book.
> *The boys*
> The boys need a book.

1. We
2. Mark and Janet
3. The women
4. You
5. Joan and I

6. My friends
7. The men
8. Mr. and Mrs. Valentine
9. I
10. They

14

B. Repeat Exercise A using the sentence "I want a sandwich."

C. Repeat Exercise A using the sentence "I have a pencil."

D. Answer these questions.

1. Do you have one book or two books?
    (I have two books.)

2. Do you have one notebook or three notebooks?

3. Do you need a pen?

4. How many pens do you need?

5. Do you have a watch?

6. What kind of watch do you have?

7. How many pencils do you want?

8. Do you have two hands?

9. How many fingers do you have?

10. Do you have three thumbs?

11. Do you want a new shirt?

12. Do you have a hat?

13. How many hats do you want?

14. Do you have many friends in this class?

IV CONVERSATION

Answer these questions.

Are these books
or pencils?

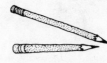

These are ___pencils___.

Are these hats
or gloves?

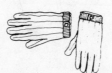

These are _oʀ gloves_

Are these shoes
or watches?

These are _____.

Are these cups
or glasses?

These are _____.

Are these doors
or windows?

These are _____.

Are these tables
or chairs?

These are _____.

Are these rugs
or flowers?

These are _____.

Are these books
or blackboards?

These are _____.

Are these shirts
or sweaters?

These are _____.

Are these curtains
or pictures?

These are _____.

Answer the questions again. This time use the contraction *they're*.

> **Example: Are these books or pencils? They're pencils.**

LESSON 6

I GRAMMAR

A. Third Person Singular

I walk	we walk
you walk	you walk
he	
she } walks	they walk
it	

B. Negative, Present Tense, *to be*

is not → isn't   are not → aren't

II PRACTICE DRILL

He walks into the room.
She walks to her chair.
He picks up his pencils.
She writes her name.

III EXERCISES

A. Choose the correct word.

1. Joe (walk, walks) into the room.
   (Joe walks into the room.)
2. The girl (look, looks) out the window.
3. I (open, opens) the door.
4. You (write, writes) your name.
5. We (pick, picks) up our notebook.
6. The students (sit, sits) on their chairs.
7. Patricia (pick, picks) up her pen.
8. Mr. Jefferson and Ms. Watson (open, opens) the window.
9. The boy and girl (walk, walks) into the room.
10. Mr. Schwartz (sit, sits) down.
11. Claude (has*, have) a pencil.
12. Sara (has, have) a red pen.
13. The teacher (walk, walks) to the door.
14. She (close, closes) the door.
15. He (look, looks) at our compositions.
16. She (pick, picks) up her pencil and (correct, corrects) our compositions.

* The third person singular of *to have* is *has.*

18

B. Write the plural of the following words.

hand _____ *hands* _____   man _____

thumb _____   room _____

picture _____   table _____

chair _____   teacher _____

girl _____   student _____

boy _____   watch _____

woman _____   shoe _____

finger _____   suit _____

child _____   foot _____

C. Read this paragraph aloud.

I walk into the room. I walk to my chair. I sit down. I pick up my pencil. I write my name.
Read the paragraph again changing *I* to *She*. (*She* walks into the room. *She* walks to *her* chair, etc.)

D. Repeat Exercise C using the pronoun *He*. (*He* walks into the room. *He* walks to *his* chair.)

E. Repeat Exercise C using the pronoun *We*.
(*We* walk into the room. *We* walk to *our* chairs.)

F. Change these sentences to the negative.*

1. This is a book.
   (This is <u>not</u> a book.)

2. These are my gloves.

3. Terry is a good student.

4. Today is Saturday.

5. Ms. Bluefeather is a teacher.

6. This is a chalkboard.

* Note to teachers: Read this exercise aloud. Have the students change the sentences as instructed, with their books closed. Follow this procedure whenever possible in subsequent exercises.

7. Gloria and Victor are students.

8. The door is open.

9. There are three books on the table.

10. This is your hat.

11. The woman is in the room.

12. This is your pencil.

13. He is busy.

14. There is a large rug on the floor.

15. They are good students.

16. She is a good friend.

G. Repeat Exercise F using the contractions *isn't* and *aren't*.

> **Example: 1. This is a book.**
>   *(This isn't a book.)*
>   2. These are my gloves.
>   *(These aren't my gloves.)*

H. Change the sentences in Exercise F to questions.

> **Example: 1. This is a book.**
>   *(Is this a book?)*
>   2. These are my gloves.
>   *(Are these my gloves?)*

LESSON 7

I GRAMMAR

A. Present Continuous Tense (-*ing* Form)

I am walking   we are walking
you are walking   you are walking
he is walking
she is walking   they are walking
it is walking

B. Contracted Form

I'm walking   we're walking
you're walking   you're walking
he's walking
she's walking   they're walking
it's walking

II PRACTICE DRILL

I am walking into the room.
I am walking to my chair.
I am sitting down.
I am picking up my pencil.
I am writing my name.

III EXERCISES

A. Substitute the words in the sentence, "I am walking."

> **Example: I am walking.**
> *He*
> He is walking.
> *You*
> You are walking.

1. He   6. We
2. Hans   7. They
3. The girl   8. The students
4. She   9. The student
5. You   10. I

B. Change the sentences to the Present Continuous.
Change *every day* to *now*.

1. I walk to the market every day.
   (I am walking to the market now.)

2. John opens the door every day.

3. Mary walks into the room every day.

4. I write in my notebook every day.

5. They sit at the table every day.

6. The girl looks out of the window every day.

7. The man walks every day.

8. The student closes the window every day.

9. We study our lesson every day.

10. Kim picks up his pencil every day.

C. Repeat Exercise B using the contracted form.

Example: 1. I walk to the market every day.
   (I'm walking to the market now.)

D. Read this paragraph aloud.

She is walking into the room. She's walking to her chair. She's sitting down. She's picking up her pencil. She's writing her name.

E. Read the paragraph again changing *she* to *he*. (*He* is walking into the room. *He's* walking to *his* chair, etc.)

F. Repeat Exercise D using the pronoun *we*. (*We* are walking into the room. *We're* walking to *our* chairs, etc.)

G. Repeat Exercise D using the pronoun *they*. (*They* are walking into the room. *They're* walking to *their* chairs, etc.)

H. Repeat Exercise D using the pronoun *you*. (*You* are walking into the room. *You're* walking to *your* chair, etc.)

IV CONVERSATION

What time is it now?
It is a quarter after twelve.

What time is it now?
It is twenty-five after twelve.

What time is it now?
It is half past twelve.

What time is it now?
It is twenty-five to one.

What time is it now?
It is a quarter to one.

What time is it now?
It's exactly one o'clock.

What time is it now?
It's one thirty.

What time is it now?

(1)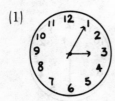

(2)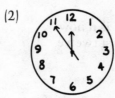

(3)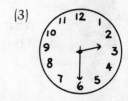

(4)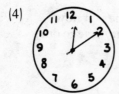

(5)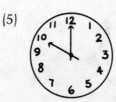

(6)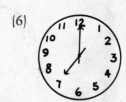

(7)

(8)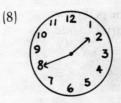

(9)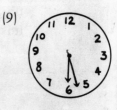

LESSON 8

I GRAMMAR

Past Tense *to be*

I was	we were
you were	you were
he was	
she was	they were
it was	

II OPPOSITES

Michael is *tall*.   Fumiko is *short*.
Tall is the opposite of *short*.
Good is the opposite of *bad*.
Yes is the opposite of *no*.

III PRACTICE DRILL

I am hungry.
I go to the cafeteria.
I buy a sandwich and a glass of milk.
I eat the sandwich.
I drink the milk.
I am not hungry.

IV EXERCISES

A. Change these sentences to the Past Tense.

  1. I am a student.
      (I was a student.)

  2. Harold Berg is a teacher.

  3. Heather is a good student.

  4. We are students.

  5. He is writing his lesson.*

  6. They are opening the windows.*

  7. The door is open.

  8. The windows and doors are open.

---

* These sentences ("He *was writing* his lessons" and "They *were opening* the windows") form the Past Continuous Tense (*-ing* Form).

25

9. The book is on the table.

10. The curtains are closed.

11. Ms. Chapman is looking out of the window.

12. Edwin is writing in his notebook.

13. This is my pencil.

14. Jefferson and Rose are also students.

15. Ms. Prouse is in the room.

16. The rug is on the floor.

17. It is 12:30.

18. Sue Ling is studying her lesson.

19. The window is closed.

20. There are flowers by the window.

B. Substitute the words in the sentence, "I was a student."

> **Example: I was a student.**
> *He*
> He was a student.
> *We*
> We were students.

1. Stanislov	6. Miss McCarthy
2. Ralph and Alex	7. We
3. You	8. She
4. They	9. Henry
5. I	10. I

C. Fill in the blanks.

1. I am ＿＿＿＿＿＿ the door.
   (I am opening the door.)

2. I am walking ＿＿＿＿＿＿ the room.
   (I am walking into the room.)

3. I am walking ＿＿＿＿＿＿ my chair.

4. I am sitting ＿＿＿＿＿＿.

5. I am _____ up my pencil.

6. I _____ my name.

D. Repeat Exercise C using the contracted form.

> **Example: I am _____ the door.**
> *(I'm opening the door.)*

E. Repeat Exercise C changing I to *she*. Use the contracted form.

> **Example: I am _____ the door.**
> *(She's opening the door.)*

V CONVERSATION

A. Answer these questions. Give only affirmative answers; begin each answer with *Yes*.

1. Are you a good student?
   (Yes, I am a good student.)

2. Is today Saturday?
   (Yes, today is Saturday.)

3. Were you in the cafeteria yesterday?

4. Are there three chairs in this room?

5. Are there books and pencils on the table?

6. Is the door open?

7. Is Miss Murphy a good teacher?

8. Is Mr. Jones in the cafeteria?

9. Was the window open yesterday?

10. Is there a rug on the floor?

11. Is Mr. Haines a teacher?

12. Are you busy today?

13. Was yesterday Sunday?

14. Were you absent from class yesterday?

15. Was your friend absent from class yesterday?

16. Are your gloves on the table?

B. Repeat the exercise above, but this time give a negative answer to each question. Begin each answer with *No*.

Example: 1. Are you a good student?
     (No, I am not a good student.)
   2. Is today Saturday?
      (No, today is not Saturday.)

I GRAMMAR

A. Short Answers

Affirmative   *Negative*

Affirmative	Negative	
Yes, I am.	No, I'm not.	
Yes, you are.	No, you're not.	No, you aren't.
Yes, he is.	No, he's not.	No, he isn't.
Yes, she is.	No, she's not.	No, she isn't.
Yes, it is.	No, it's not.	No, it isn't.
Yes, we are.	No, we're not.	No, we aren't.
Yes, you are.	No, you're not.	No, you aren't.
Yes, they are.	No, they're not.	No, they aren't.

B. Past Tense

Affirmative	Negative
Yes, I was.	No, I wasn't.
Yes, you were.	No, you weren't.
Yes, he was.	No, he wasn't.
Yes, she was.	No, she wasn't.
Yes, it was.	No, it wasn't.
Yes, we were.	No, we weren't.
Yes, you were.	No, you weren't.
Yes, they were.	No, they weren't.

II PRACTICE DRILL

Are you a student? Yes, I am.
Are you a teacher? No, I'm not.
Are you students? Yes, we are.
Are you teachers? No, we're not.
Are you teachers? No, we aren't.
Was Alicia late? Yes, she was. No, she wasn't.
Were the Flood children here today? Yes, they were. No, they weren't.

III EXERCISES

A. Answer these questions using short affirmative answers.

1. Are you a good student?
   (Yes, I am.)

2. Is today Tuesday?
   (Yes, it is.)

3. Are there three chairs in this room?
   (Yes, there are.)

4. Is the door open?

5. Is Ms. Garcia a good teacher?

6. Is Mr. Hernandez in the cafeteria?

7. Is there a rug on the floor?

8. Are you busy today?

9. Are your gloves on the table?

10. Is your name Peter?

11. Are we in a classroom?

12. Are we studying English?

13. Are Jennifer and Jessica in school today?

14. Are you studying English?

B. Repeat Exercise A using short negative answers. Use both types.

Example: 1. Are you a good student?
   (No, I'm not.)
2. Is today Tuesday?
   (No, it's not./No, It isn't.)
3. Are there three chairs in this room?
   (No, there aren't.)

C. Answer these Past Tense questions using short affirmative answers.

1. Were you in the cafeteria yesterday?
   (Yes, I was.)

2. Was yesterday Wednesday?
   (Yes, it was.)

3. Was the window open yesterday?

4. Were you absent from class yesterday?

5. Was Victor in class yesterday?

6. Was the dog in the room yesterday?

7. Were we late for class today?

8. Were we studying English yesterday?

9. Were you and your sister living in Brazil?

10. Were Mr. and Mrs. Corrigan in class yesterday?

11. Were the boys and the girls walking into the room?

12. Was Ivan in his room today?

D. Repeat Exercise C using short negative answers.

> **Example: 1. Were you in the cafeteria yesterday?**
> *(No, I wasn't.)*
> 2. Was yesterday Wednesday?
> *(No, it wasn't.)*

IV CONVERSATION

Answer these questions. Use short answers.

1. Are you a student?

2. Are you a good student?

3. Are you a teacher?

4. Is your room big? Is it small?

5. Is your friend tall? Is your friend short?

6. Am I a teacher? Am I a student?

7. Were you late today?

8. Is today Saturday? Monday?

9. Was yesterday Sunday? Tuesday?

10. Is this our classroom?

11. Were we good in class today?

12. Are we in the English class now?

13. Are Mr. and Mrs. Adams in class today?

14. Are the students in the room now?

15. Is your teacher by the window?

LESSON 10

I GRAMMAR

Past Tense

A. Regular Verbs

Present	Past
walk	walked
open	opened
pick	picked
look	looked
close	closed

B. Irregular Verbs

Present	Past
sit	sat
write	wrote
read	read
drink	drank
have	had
eat	ate
buy	bought
come	came
get	got
go	went

II OPPOSITES

Tall is the opposite of *short*.
Good is the opposite of *bad*.
Yes is the opposite of *no*.
In is the opposite of *out*.
Up is the opposite of *down*.
Happy is the opposite of *sad*.
Late is the opposite of *early*.
Big is the opposite of *little* (or *small*).
Hot is the opposite of *cold*.

III EXERCISES

A. Change these sentences to Past Tense.

1. I walk into the room.
    (I <u>walked</u> into the room.)

33

2. John opens the window.

3. Miss Foley writes her name.

4. You have a pencil.

5. We close the door.

6. Mary sits on her chair.

7. Mr. Jones eats a sandwich.

8. The man buys a new suit.

9. The teacher reads the book.

10. The girl drinks a glass of milk.

B. Substitute the words in the sentence, "I walked into the room yesterday."

> **Example: I walked into the room yesterday.**
> *He*
> He walked into the room yesterday.
> *You*
> You walked into the room yesterday.

1. He
2. You
3. The cat
4. She
5. We

6. They
7. Carla and Sophia
8. The dog and cat
9. You
10. I

C. Fill in the blanks.

1. *Tall* is the opposite of _____*short*_____.

2. _____ is the opposite of *no*.

3. *In* is the opposite of _____ .

4. *Sad* is the opposite of _____ .

5. _____ is the opposite of *cold*.

6. _____ is the opposite of *late*.

7. *Good* is the opposite of _____ .

8. *Up* is the opposite of _____ .

9. *Little* is the opposite of _____ .

10. _____ is the opposite of *happy*.

D. Read this paragraph aloud.

I am hungry. I go to the cafeteria. I buy a sandwich and a glass of milk. I eat the sandwich. I drink the milk. I am not hungry.

Read the paragraph changing *I* to *Helen*. (*Helen is* hungry. *Helen goes* to the cafeteria, etc.)

E. Repeat Exercise D using the Past Tense. (I *was* hungry. I *went* to the cafeteria, etc.)

F. Repeat Exercise D using the Past Tense and the pronoun *We*. (*We were* hungry. *We went* to the cafeteria, etc.)

IV CONVERSATION

A. Answer these questions.

1. What is the opposite of *tall*?
   (*The opposite of <u>tall</u> is <u>short</u>.*)

2. What is *good* the opposite of?
   (<u>Good</u> *is the opposite of <u>bad</u>.*)

3. What is the opposite of *sad*?

4. What is *no* the opposite of?

5. What is the opposite of *down*?

6. What is *out* the opposite of?

7. What is the opposite of *short*?

8. What is *big* the opposite of?

9. What is the opposite of *up*?

10. What is *in* the opposite of?

11. What is the opposite of *bad*?

12. What is *early* the opposite of?

B. Answer these questions.

1. What is the plural form of the word *book*?
   (The plural form of the word book *is* books.)

2. What is the plural form of the word *man*?

3. What is the plural form of the word *woman*?

4. What is the plural form of the word *boy*?

5. What is the plural of *shoe*? of *pencil*? of *girl*? of *watch*? of *table*? of *glass*?*

C. What time is it?

(1)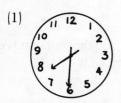

(2)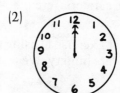

(3)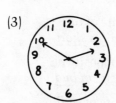

(4)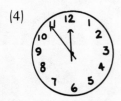

(5)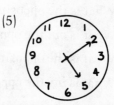

---

* Nouns ending in an *s* sound (s, z, ch, sh, x) add -*es* to form the plural. The -*es* is pronounced as a separate syllable. (Examples: one watch, two *watches*; one box, two *boxes*; one glass, two *glasses*.)

LESSON 11

I GRAMMAR

Object Pronouns

* Subject Pronoun	Object Pronoun	Subject Pronoun	Object Pronoun
I	me	we	us
you	you	you	you
he	him	they	them
she	her		
it	it		

II PRACTICE DRILL

A. I go to school with Sergio every day.
>   I go with him.
>   He goes with me.

I see Ruth on the bus every day.
>   I see her.
>   She sees me.

Melina sits near Edgar and me at the lesson.
>   She sits near us.
>   We sit near her.

I see Adam and Grace at school every day.
>   I see them.
>   They see me.

You walked your dog yesterday.
>   You walked it.
>   It walked with you.

B. I get up at eight o'clock.

>   I wash my face.
>   I comb my hair.
>   I put on my clothes.
>   I eat my breakfast.
>   I put on my hat and coat.
>   I go to work.

* Subject pronouns are used as subjects of the verb; object pronouns are used as direct or indirect objects of the verb, and as objects of prepositions.

37

III EXERCISES

A. Choose the correct word.

1. I go with (he, him) to school every day.
   (I go with <u>him</u> to school every day.)

2. She sits near (we, us).

3. I see (she, her) in the cafeteria every day.

4. I walk with (them, they) to school.

5. They study with (us, we).

6. I eat with (she, her) in the cafeteria.

7. He walks to school with (me, I) every day.

8. She speaks to (we, us) in English.

9. I open the door for (she, her).

10. Muriel opens the door for (I, me).

B. Change these sentences to Past Tense.

1. Tom and Martha are students.
   (Tom and Martha <u>were</u> students.)

2. The boys eat sandwiches.
   (The boys <u>ate</u> sandwiches.)

3. Ms. Aaron walks into the room.

4. A woman opens the door.

5. The girl sits on her chair.

6. There is a magazine on the table.

7. Mr. May is a good teacher.

8. The windows are open.

9. We have four pencils.

10. The man looks out the window.

11. Mary buys two apples.

12. There are two strange men in John's office.

13. I drink milk.

38

14. The boy picks up his watch.

15. You write your name.

16. Ms. Ryan and Mr. Jones are hungry.

17. The boys come home after school.

C. Repeat Exercise B using subject pronouns and the Past Tense.

> **Example: 1. Tom and Martha are students.**
> *(They were students.)*

IV CONVERSATION

A. Answer these questions.

1. Where do you live?
2. When did you come here?
3. Where do you study your lessons?
4. When did you get up this morning?
5. Where do you work?

B. Look at this picture and answer the questions.

I. VanRynbach

1. Where is the rug?
2. Where are the pictures?
3. Where is the big chair?
4. Where is the table?

5. Where is the window?
6. Is there a table in your classroom? Where is it?
7. Is there a book in your classroom? Where is it?
8. Is there a pencil in your classroom? Where is it?
9. Are there chairs in your classroom? Where are they?
10. Is there a chalkboard in your classroom? Where is it?
11. Are there students in your classroom? Where are they?
12. Is there a clock in your classroom? Where is it? What time is it?

LESSON 12

I GRAMMAR

A. Articles *a, an**

Use *an* before a word with a vowel sound (**a, e, i, o**, and **u**)

a sandwich	*an* apple
a European	*an* English home
a glass of milk	*an* American
a cafeteria	*an* orange
a boy	*an* umbrella
a hungry girl	*an* hour

B. Prepositions: **in, into, on, of, to, after, before, up.**

II PRACTICE DRILL

I walk into the kitchen.
I am in the kitchen.
I wash before I eat.
I go to the table.
I eat a sandwich.
I drink a glass of milk.
I pick up an apple.
I put it on the table.
I eat the apple.
After I eat, I wash the dishes.

III EXERCISES

A. Fill in the blanks.

1. You are _____ Brazilian.
   (You are a̲ Brazilian.)

2. Your teacher is _____ American.
   (Your teacher is a̲n̲ American.)

3. Miss Dutra is _____ student.

4. Yesterday Serge bought _____ suit.

5. Ada has _____ umbrella.

---

* *A* and *an* are indefinite, referring unspecifically to singular nouns. *The* is definite, referring to a particular noun, and is used with both singular and plural nouns. (I would like to have *a* sandwich. *The* sandwich you made for me is good.)

41

6. I eat _____ apple for lunch every day.

7. He is _____ old man.

8. Fred is _____ good boy.

9. This is _____ easy exercise.

10. She is _____ hungry girl.

11. Mr. Essig is _____ good teacher.

12. Is Ms. Niles _____ Argentine?

B. Fill in the blanks with *in, on, of, to, after, before, up,* or *at.*

1. There are two pictures _____ the wall.
   (There are two pictures <u>on</u> the wall.)

2. There are four chairs _____ this room.

3. How many books are there _____ the table?

4. Mary walked _____ her chair.

5. The blackboard is _____ the wall.

6. The boy drank a glass _____ milk.

7. The student goes _____ the cafeteria.

8. You have a glove _____ your hand.

9. Donna washes _____ she eats.

10. Your lesson begins _____ eight o'clock.

11. It is a quarter _____ twelve.

12. He always sits _____ this seat.

13. There is a rug _____ the floor.

14. Tall is the opposite _____ short.

15. The teacher writes _____ the blackboard.

16. I put _____ my hat and coat.

17. I get _____ at eight o'clock every morning.

18. John picked _____ the pencil which was on the floor.

19. _____ I washed the apple, I ate it.

42

LESSON 13

I GRAMMAR

Present Tense Questions

do I walk	do we walk
do you walk	do you walk
does he walk	
does she walk	do they walk
does it walk	

II PRACTICAL INFORMATION

Ordinal Numbers

one	first	six	sixth
two	second	seven	seventh
three	third	eight	eighth
four	fourth	nine	ninth
five	fifth	ten	tenth

III PRACTICE DRILL

A. They get on the bus.
    They pay their fare.
    They go to their seats.
    They sit down.
    They ride to work.
    They get off the bus.

B. There are seven days in the week.
    The days of the week are Sunday, Monday, Tuesday, Wednes-
    day, Thursday, Friday, and Saturday.
    Sunday is the first day of the week.
    Monday is the second day of the week.
    Saturday is the last day of the week.
    Sunday comes before Monday.
    Tuesday comes before Wednesday.
    Thursday comes after Wednesday.
    Friday comes after Thursday.

IV EXERCISES

A. Change these statements to questions. Begin each question
    with "Do you . . ."

1. I study English every day.
   (Do you study English every day?)

2. I work on Sunday.

3. I speak English well.

4. I walk to my work.

5. I live in the United States.

6. I read the newspaper every day.

7. I write in my notebook every day.

8. I like to study English.

9. I eat in the cafeteria.

10. I speak French.

11. I look out the window.

12. I comb and brush my hair every morning.

13. I write all the new words in my notebook.

14. I go to the movies once a week.

15. I watch television almost every night.

16. I know Mr. and Mrs. Reeves very well.

B. Change these statements to questions. Begin each question with "Does he . . ." or "Does she . . ."

1. He lives in Boston.
   (Does he live in Boston?)

2. She works with Mr. May.

3. He speaks English well.

4. Michael walks to work.

5. She reads the newspaper every day.

6. Claudia writes in her notebook every day.

7. She likes to study English.

8. Mr. Rocca eats in the cafeteria.

9. He speaks French.

10. Bernie lives in Washington.

11. Stefanie watches television every night.

12. He goes to work by bus.

13. She looks up all the new words in her dictionary.

14. He combs his hair every morning.

C. Substitute the words in the sentence, "Do you study English every day?"

Example: Do you study English every day?
> *we*
> Do we study English every day?
> *he*
> Does he study English every day?

---

1. he		6. Ari	
2. Louis		7. Beth and Billie	
3. you		8. they	
4. I		9. she	
5. Sally		10. we	

V CONVERSATION

Answer these questions.

1. How many days are there in a week?

2. What are the days of the week?

3. What is the first day of the week?

4. What is the last day of the week?

5. What is the second day of the week?

6. What is the third day of the week?

7. What day comes before Tuesday?

8. What day comes after Tuesday?

9. What day comes before Thursday?

10. What day comes after Thursday?

11. Are you the first child born in your family?

12. What is the name of the second child born in your family?

13. Is this your first class in English?

LESSON 14

I GRAMMAR

Present Tense Negatives *do not (don't), does not (doesn't)*

Full Form	*Contracted Form*
I do not study	I don't study
you do not study	you don't study
he does not study	he doesn't study
she does not study	she doesn't study
it does not study	it doesn't study
we do not study	we don't study
you do not study	you don't study
they do not study	they don't study

Yes, I do	No, I don't	Yes, we do	No, we don't
Yes, you do	No, you don't	Yes, you do	No, you don't
Yes, he does	No, he doesn't		
Yes, she does	No, she doesn't	Yes, they do	No, they don't
Yes, it does	No, it doesn't		

II PRACTICAL INFORMATION

Months of the Year

January	April	July	October
February	May	August	November
March	June	September	December

III PRACTICE DRILL

A. They get on the bus.
    They pay their fare.
    They go to their seats.
    They sit down.
    They ride to work.
    They get off the bus.

Change the above to the negative.
(They do not get on the bus.)
(They do not pay their fare.)

Change the above to the negative using contractions.
(They don't get on the bus.)
(They don't pay their fare.)

B. There are twelve months in a year.
The first month of the year is January.
The second month of the year is February.
The third month is March.
The last month is December.
January comes before February.
February comes before March.
May comes after April.
June comes after May.

IV EXERCISES

A. Answer these questions using complete sentences after short negative answers.

1. Do you work on Sunday?
(No, I don't. <u>I don't</u> work on Sunday.)

2. Do you speak French?

3. Do you study English every day?

4. Do you speak English well?

5. Do you walk to your work?

6. Do you live in Boston?

7. Do you read the newspaper every day?

8. Do you write in your notebook every day?

9. Do you like to study English?

10. Do you eat in the cafeteria?

11. Do you pay your fare on the bus?

12. Do you ride to your work?

13. Do you write all the new words in your notebook?

14. Do you watch television every night?

15. Do you get up early every morning?

16. Do you go to the movies very often?

B. Repeat Exercise A using only short answers, negative or affirmative.

> **Example: 1. Do you work on Sunday?**
> *(Yes, I do.)*
> 2. Do you speak French?
> *(No, I don't.)*

C. Answer these questions using complete sentences after short negative answers.

1. Does she speak English?
   (No, she doesn't. She doesn't speak English.)

2. Does he work on Sunday?
   (No, he doesn't. He doesn't work on Sunday.)

3. Does she live with you?

4. Does your friend speak English well?

5. Does your teacher speak French?

6. Does he walk to work?

7. Does she walk to work?

8. Does your friend eat in the cafeteria at noon?

9. Does your friend like to study?

10. Does he live in America?

11. Does Helen like to watch television?

12. Does John go to the park with you on Sundays?

13. Does Mr. Smith go to work by bus?

D. Repeat Exercise C using only short answers, negative and affirmative.

> **Example: 1. Does she speak English?**
> *(Yes, she does.)*
> 2. Does he work on Sunday?
> *(No, he doesn't.)*

V CONVERSATION

Answer these questions.

1. How many months are there in a year?
2. What are the months of the year?
3. What is the first month of the year?
4. What is the second month?
5. What is the third month?
6. What is the last month?
7. What month comes before February?
8. What month comes before March?
9. What month comes after April?
10. What month comes after May?
11. How many days are there in a week?
12. What are the days of the week?
13. What day is today?
14. What day was yesterday?

LESSON 15

I GRAMMAR

Past Tense

Present	Past	Present	Past
wash	washed	like	liked
comb	combed	put	put
study	studied	speak	spoke
work	worked	tell	told
live	lived	pay	paid

II OPPOSITES

This pencil is *short*.   This pencil is *long*.

Short is the opposite of *long*.

The opposite of *hot* is *cold*.
The opposite of *in* is *out*.
The opposite of *black* is *white*.
The opposite of *many* is *few*.
The opposite of *before* is *after*.
The opposite of *easy* is *difficult*.

III PRACTICAL INFORMATION

The Seasons

spring   **autumn (fall)**
summer   **winter**

There are four seasons in a year.
Spring comes before summer.
Summer comes before autumn.
Autumn comes before winter.
Winter comes before spring.
In winter it is cold.
In autumn it is cool.
In spring it is warm.
In summer it is hot.

A. Change these sentences to the Past Tense.

   1. Peter washes the dishes.
       (Peter <u>washed</u> the dishes.)

   2. Marie gets up at 7 o'clock every day.

   3. I comb my hair several times a day.

   4. The girl puts on her shoes.

   5. He always comes to his lesson on time.

   6. Eleanor studies her lesson well.

   7. The boy likes English.

   8. We live in New York.

   9. The women work every day.

   10. We pay our fare on the bus.

   11. The boys study English and French.

   12. They come to work by bus.

   13. He gets up early every morning.

   14. John puts on his hat before he puts on his coat.

   15. We like our English teacher very much.

B. Add the words to the sentences and make any other necessary changes.

   1. He comes to class early.
       a. now   *(He <u>is coming</u> to class <u>now</u>.)*
       b. yesterday   *(He <u>came</u> to class <u>yesterday</u>.)*
       c. every day   *(He <u>comes</u> to class <u>every day</u>.)*

   2. John lives in New York.
       a. last year
       b. now
       c. every July

   3. Mr. Bradley goes to work.
       a. now
       b. every day
       c. last week

54

4. Mary speaks English.
    a. last night
    b. now
    c. every day

5. He put on his coat.
    a. last night
    b. now
    c. every day

6. Mr. and Mrs. O'Brien work hard.
    a. yesterday
    b. every day
    c. now

C. Write the opposites.

up ___*down*___   in _____   past _____

short _____   cold _____   easy _____

white _____   tall _____   good _____

black _____   yes _____   few _____

before _____   after _____   bad _____

out _____   many _____   off _____

D. Answer these questions.

1. What is the opposite of *short*?
    (The opposite of short is tall.)

2. What is the opposite of *black*?

3. What is the opposite of *many*?

4. What is the opposite of *after*?

5. What is the opposite of *difficult*?

6. What is the opposite of *in*?

7. What is the opposite of *hot*?

E. Read this paragraph aloud.

He gets on the bus. He pays his fare. He goes to a seat. He sits down. He rides to work. He gets off the bus.

Read the paragraph again changing the tense from Present to Past.
(He *got* on the bus. He *paid his* fare, etc.)

F. Repeat Exercise E using the Past Tense and the pronoun *you*.
(*You got* on the bus. *You paid your* fare, etc.)

G. Repeat Exercise E using the Past Tense and the pronoun *they*.
(*They got* on the bus. *They paid their* fares, etc.)

V CONVERSATION

Answer these questions.

1. How many seasons are there in a year?
2. What are the seasons of the year?
3. What season comes before summer?
4. What season comes after summer?
5. What season comes before autumn?
6. What season comes after autumn?
7. What season comes before winter?
8. What season comes after winter?
9. What season comes before spring?
10. What season comes after spring?

11. Is it hot or cold in winter?

12. Is it hot or cold in summer?

13. Is it warm or cold in spring?

14. Is it cool or hot in autumn?

15. Which season of the year do you like best?

LESSON 16

I GRAMMAR

Past Tense Questions

did I study	did we study
did you study	did you study
did he study	
did she study	did they study
did it study	

II PRACTICAL INFORMATION

Colors*

Black	Blue	Orange
White	Green	Brown
Yellow	Red	

Ink is black.   Snow is white.
The paper is white.   The sky is blue.
Grass is green.   The sun is yellow.
The tree is brown.   The apple is red.

III OPPOSITES

Yes is the opposite of *no*.   *First* is the opposite of *last*.
Push is the opposite of *pull*. *Little* is the opposite of *big*.

IV PRACTICE DRILL

I pick up my pen.
I write a letter to my friend.
I tell my friend I am well.
I tell him I like the United States.
I sign my name.
I fold the letter and put it into an envelope.
I address the envelope.

V EXERCISES

A. Change to questions. Begin each question with "Did you . . ."

   1. I studied English yesterday.
      (Did you study English yesterday?)

---

* Refer to the color chart on the back cover of this book.

2. I walked to work this morning.

3. I ate in the cafeteria.

4. I studied French.

5. I walked in the park yesterday.

6. I lived in Boston.

7. I read the newspaper this morning.

8. I wrote in my notebook yesterday.

9. I spoke to Mr. Smith yesterday.

10. I worked yesterday.

11. I combed my hair.

12. I walked to work.

13. I learned many new words yesterday.

14. I looked up all the new words in my dictionary.

B. Change to questions. Begin each question with "Did he . . ."
or "Did she . . ."

1. He studied English yesterday.
   (Did he study English yesterday?)

2. She walked to work.

3. He ate in the cafeteria.

4. She studied French.

5. Alan lived in Los Angeles.

6. He read the newspaper this morning.

7. Ms. Sommers wrote in her notebook yesterday.

8. He spoke to Mildred.

9. She walked in the park.

10. He liked French.

11. She put the books on the desk.

12. Pat came to school by bus.

C. Answer these questions.

1. Is this ink black or white?
   (It's black.)

2. Is the sun green or yellow?

3. Is grass green or red?

4. Is paper black or white?

5. Is snow white or green?

6. Is the pencil brown or white?

7. Is the sky green or blue?

8. Is an apple blue or red?

D. Using the color chart on the back of this book, ask questions about the colors and answer them.

Examples: 1. (Pointing) What color is this?
   It's brown.
2. (Pointing) What's that color?
   That's blue.

VI CONVERSATION

Answer these questions.

1. What color is the ink?
   (The ink is black.) or *(It's black.)*

2. What color is snow?

3. What color is the sky?

4. What color is the sun?

5. What color is your pencil?

6. What color is your book?

7. What color are your shoes?

8. What color is your coat?

9. What color are your eyes?

10. What color are your friend's eyes?

LESSON 17

A. Past Tense Negative *did not (didn't)*

Full Form	*Contracted form*
I did not study	I didn't study
you did not study	you didn't study
he did not study	he didn't study
she did not study	she didn't study
it did not study	it didn't study
we did not study	we didn't study
you did not study	you didn't study
they did not study	they didn't study

B. Short Answers—Past Tense

Affirmative	*Negative*
Yes, I did.	No, I didn't.
Yes, you did.	No, you didn't.
Yes, he did.	No, he didn't.
Yes, she did.	No, she didn't.
Yes, it did.	No, it didn't.
Yes, we did.	No, we didn't.
Yes, you did.	No, you didn't.
Yes, they did.	No, they didn't.

II PRACTICE DRILL

A. I went to the post office.
    I stood at the stamp window.
    I bought a stamp for my letter.
    I put the stamp on the envelope.
    I mailed the letter in the mailbox.

B. A person has two eyes.
    A person has one mouth.
    A person has one nose.
    A person has two ears.
    A person has two hands.
    A person has two feet.

C. A woman sees with her eyes.
    A woman eats with her mouth.
    A woman smells with her nose.

A man hears with his ears.
A man feels with his hands.
A man walks with his feet.

III EXERCISES

A. Answer these questions using "No, I did not . . ."

1. Did you work yesterday?
(No, I did not work yesterday.)

2. Did you study English yesterday?

3. Did you walk to work yesterday?

4. Did you study last night?

5. Did you eat at home this morning?

6. Did you write in your notebook yesterday?

7. Did you read the newspaper this morning?

8. Did you go to the movies last night?

9. Did you like your lesson yesterday?

10. Did you talk to your friend yesterday?

11. Did you pay your fare on the bus?

12. Did you come to school by bus?

13. Did you watch television last night?

14. Did you put away your books after the lesson?

B. Repeat Exercise A using the contracted form. Use short negative answers followed by complete sentences.

> **Example: 1. Did you work yesterday?**
> *(No, I didn't. I didn't work yesterday.)*

C. Answer these questions using "No, he did not . . ." and "No, she did not . . ."

1. Did your friend work yesterday?
(No, he did not work yesterday.)

2. Did your father come with you?

3. Did your sister come with you?

4. Did your friend study English yesterday?

5. Did he study English in Europe?

6. Did your teacher walk to work yesterday?

7. Did John eat in the cafeteria this morning?

8. Did Mary eat in the cafeteria this morning?

9. Did your friend read the newspaper?

10. Did your friend walk to work this morning?

11. Did Mr. Shaw put on his coat?

12. Did Ms. Riley like Washington?

13. Did Henry wait for you yesterday?

14. Did he buy the book?

D. Repeat Exercise C using the contracted form. Use short negative answers followed by complete sentences.

> **Example: 1. Did your friend work yesterday?**
> *(No, she didn't. She didn't work yesterday.)*
> **2. Did your father come with you?**
> *(No, he didn't. He didn't come with me.)*

E. Repeat Exercise C using only short affirmative answers.

> **Example: 1. Did your friend work yesterday?**
> *(Yes, she did.)*
> **2. Did your father come with you?**
> *(Yes, he did.)*

F. Read this paragraph aloud.

She went to the post office. She stood at the stamp window. She bought a stamp for her letter. She put the stamp on the envelope. She mailed the letter in the mailbox.

Read the paragraph again changing to the negative. Use the contracted form.
(She *didn't go* to the post office. She *didn't stand* at the stamp window, etc.)

G. Fill in the blanks.

1. A boy _____ with his eyes.
   (A boy sees with his eyes.)

2. A boy eats with his _____ .

3. A boy smells with his _____ .

4. A girl _____ with her ears.

5. A girl _____ with her hands.

6. A girl walks with her _____ .

IV CONVERSATION

Answer these questions.

1. What do people see with?
   (They see with their eyes.)

2. What do you eat with?

3. What do people smell with?

4. What do people walk with?

5. What do you feel with?

6. What do you hear with?

LESSON 18

I GRAMMAR

A. Past Tense Verbs

Regular		Irregular	
Present	*Past*	*Present*	*Past*
sign	signed	stand	stood
fold	folded	sell	sold
address	addressed	take	took
smell	smelled	give	gave
mail	mailed	see	saw
walk	walked	hear	heard
talk	talked	feel	felt

B. Adjectives

Black ink
White paper
Green grass
Brown pencil
White snow

An **easy** lesson
The **hot** coffee
An **early** class
A **happy** boy
The **short** pencil

Use an adjective before the word it describes.

II OPPOSITES

The opposite of *black* is *white*.
The opposite of *easy* is *difficult.*

The opposite of *early* is *late.*
The opposite of *sell* is *buy.*
The opposite of *start* is *stop.*
The opposite of *day* is *night.*

III EXERCISES

A. Change these sentences to Past Tense.

1. I pay my fare on the bus.
   (I *paid* my fare on the bus.)

2. John folds the piece of paper.

3. Mr. Smith addresses a letter to his brother.

4. You sign your name.

5. We ride on the bus every day.

6. The woman tells her son she is well and happy.

7. The little girls sees her friend every day.

8. Mary hears the concert.

9. The girls smell the perfume.

10. The boys go to school by bus.

11. She feels the package with her hands.

12. We see each other once a week.

13. John tells me all his troubles.

14. We go to the movies every Saturday night.

15. I hear someone in the next room.

B. Add an adjective before the *italicized word.*

1. The *ink* is on the table.
   (The <u>red ink</u> is on the table.)

2. The *book* is on the desk.

3. The boy drank a glass of *milk.*

4. The *teacher* ate in the cafeteria.

5. The coat is on the *chair.*

6. There are students in the *room.*

7. There is a *stamp* on the envelope.

8. There is a *package* in the room.

C. Fill in the blanks.

The opposite of **sell** is
_____*buy*_____ .

The opposite of _____
is **night.**

The opposite of **easy** is
_____ .

The opposite of _____
is **late.**

The opposite of _____
is **white.**

The opposite of _____
is **stop.**

D. Fill in the blanks with appropriate prepositions.

1. You see _____ your eyes.
   (You see <u>with</u> your eyes.)

2. We walk _____ work every day.

3. She sat _____ the chair.

4. Omar eats _____ the cafeteria.

5. Gina put the letter _____ an envelope.

6. How many months are there _____ a year?

7. January comes _____ February.

8. It doesn't come _____ February.

9. The woman gets _____ the bus and walks _____ her apartment.

E. Read this paragraph aloud.

I went to the post office. I stood at the stamp window. I bought a stamp for my letter. I put the stamp on my envelope. I mailed the letter.

Read the paragraph again changing to the negative. Use the contracted form.
(I *didn't go* to the post office. I *didn't stand* at the stamp window. etc.)

F. Repeat Exercise E changing to the Present Tense.

(I *go* to the post office. I *stand* at the stamp window, etc.)

IV CONVERSATION

1. What color is snow? Is it ever black?

2. What season is it hot in your country? What season is it cold?

3. What is the opposite of *open?*

4. Is January the first or last month of the year?

5. Which month is the sixth month of the year? The tenth?

6. Does February come before or after January?

7. Is that office building very big or very small?

8. Is this exercise easy or difficult?

9. When do you study? Where?

10. Are there many students in your class? Are there few?

11. What is the opposite of *pull*?

12. Is December a warm month or a cold month?

13. Is coal black or white?

14. Do you have a son or a daughter?

15. What is the opposite of *down*?

16. Are lemons sweet or sour?

17. Is your friend short or tall?

18. Were you late or early for your lesson today?

19. What is the opposite of *before*?

20. Is Mr. Reese a tall man or a short man?

LESSON 19

I GRAMMAR

Future Tense *to be*

Full Form	*Contracted Form*
I will be*	I'll be
you will be	you'll be
he will be	he'll be
she will be	she'll be
it will be	it'll be
we will be*	we'll be
you will be	you'll be
they will be	they'll be

II PRACTICAL INFORMATION

A. Numbers

11 eleven	18 eighteen	60 sixty
12 twelve	19 nineteen	70 seventy
13 thirteen	20 twenty	80 eighty
14 fourteen	21 twenty-one	90 ninety
15 fifteen	30 thirty	100 one hundred
16 sixteen	40 forty	101 one hundred one
17 seventeen	50 fifty	

Two *plus* two equals four.
Three *minus* one equals two.
Three *times* three equals nine.

B. Money

One cent is a *penny.*	$0.01	1¢
Five cents is a *nickel.*	$0.05	5¢
Ten cents is a *dime.*	$0.10	10¢
Twenty-five cents is a *quarter.*	$0.25	25¢
Fifty cents is a *half dollar.*	$0.50	50¢
One hundred cents is a *dollar.*	$1.00	100¢

III PRACTICE DRILL

A. I went to the grocery store.
   I asked the clerk for a loaf of bread and a pound of butter.

* In the past, *shall* was used in the 1st person (I, we) and *will* was used in the
2nd and 3rd person. Most people today, however, use *will* in all persons.

69

The clerk sold me the bread and butter.
She told me my bill was two dollars and fifty cents ($2.50).
I gave her a ten-dollar bill ($10).
She gave me my change.
I took the package and went home.

B. There are sixty seconds in a minute.
There are sixty minutes in an hour.
There are twenty-four hours in a day.
There are seven days in a week.
There are four weeks in a month.
There are twelve months in a year.
There are three hundred sixty-five days in a year.

IV EXERCISES

A. Change these sentences to the Future Tense.

1. He is in the cafeteria.
   (He will be in the cafeteria.)

2. They are on the second floor.

3. She is your new teacher.

4. It is warm.

5. You are very busy.

6. Glenn is a good student.

7. The book is open on the desk.

8. I am in the second class.

9. It is three o'clock.

10. Ellen and Barry are in the cafeteria.

11. She is in Chicago.

12. He is a big boy.

13. She is a good worker.

14. This is your room.

15. There is a new student in our class.

16. There are many students absent from class.

B. Repeat Exercise A using the contracted form of the Future Tense.

> **Example: 1. He is in the cafeteria.**
> *(He'll be in the cafeteria.)*

C. Fill in the blanks with the words for the numbers.

1. This is Lesson _____ .
   (This is Lesson Nineteen.)

2. The last lesson was Lesson _____ .

3. February has _____ days.

4. There are _____ months in a year.

5. There are _____ days in September.

6. There are _____ days in October.

7. The young man is _____ years old.

8. This is page _____ .

D. Answer these questions.

1. How much is two plus three?
   (Two plus three equals five.)

2. How much is four plus five? Six plus two?

3. How much is six minus three?

4. How much is ten minus five? Eight minus four?

5. How much is two times three?

6. How much is three times four? Two times six?

E. Repeat Exercise D changing the word *equals* to *is*.

> **Example: 1. How much is two plus three?**
> *(Two plus three is five.)*

F. Fill in the blanks.

1. There are _____ seconds in a minute.
   (There are <u>sixty</u> seconds in a minute.)

2. There are _____ minutes in an hour.

3. There are twenty-four hours in a _____ .

4. There are _____ weeks in a month.

5. There are twelve months in a _____ .

6. There are _____ days in a year.

V CONVERSATION

Answer these questions.

1. How many seconds are there in a minute?

2. How many minutes are there in an hour?

3. How many hours are there in a day?

4. How many days are there in a week?

5. How many weeks are there in a month?

6. How many weeks are there in a year?

7. How many months are there in a year?

8. How many days are there in a year?

9. How many students are there in your class?

10. How many days are there in the month of September? In the month of February? In the month of June?

11. How much is four quarters?

12. How much is a dime and a nickel?

13. How much is two dimes and a nickel?

14. How much is five pennies?

15. How much is a quarter, two dimes, and a nickel?

16. How much money do you have in your pocket?

LESSON 20

I GRAMMAR

A. Future Tense

Full Form	*Contracted Form*
I will study	I'll study
you will study	you'll study
he will study	he'll study
she will study	she'll study
it will study	it'll study
we will study	we'll study
you will study	you'll study
they will study	they'll study

B. Prepositions

Is the pen under the table?
   No, it isn't.
Is the pen beside the table?
   No, it isn't.
Is the pen on the table.
   Yes, it is.
Where is the pen?
   It is on the table.

II PRACTICE DRILL

We went to the grocery store.
We asked the clerk for a loaf of bread and a pound of butter.
The clerk sold us the bread and butter.
He told us our bill was two dollars and fifty cents ($2.50).
We gave him a ten-dollar bill ($10).
He gave us our change.
We took the package and went home.

III EXERCISES

A. Change these sentences to the Future Tense.

1. He works on this floor
   (He will work on this floor.)

2. She studies English every day.

3. John eats in the cafeteria.

4. I walk to my office.

5. She speaks English well.

6. John comes to his lesson early.

7. He brings his friend to class.

8. He goes to Chicago every month.

9. He studies in our class.

10. He opens the door for us.

11. He studies very much.

12. We write many compositions.

B. Repeat Exercise A using the contracted form.

> **Example: 1. He works on this floor.**
> *(He'll work on this floor.)*

C. Read this paragraph aloud.

I went to the grocery store. I asked the clerk for a loaf of bread and a pound of butter. She sold me the bread and butter. She told me my bill was two dollars and fifty cents ($2.50). I gave her a ten-dollar bill ($10). She gave me my change. I took the package and went home.

Read the paragraph again changing the tense from Past to Present.
(I go to the grocery store. etc.)

D. Repeat Exercise C changing the tense to Future. Use the contracted form.

(I'll go to the grocery store. etc.)

IV CONVERSATION

Is the pen on the table?
Is the pen under the table?
Is the pen beside the table?
Where is the pen?
Where is the table?

Is the pen on the books?
Is the pen under the books?
Are the books under the pen?
Is the pen between the books?
Where is the pen?

Is the blackboard in front of the table?
Is the blackboard beside the table?
Is the table behind the blackboard?
Is the table in front of the blackboard?
Where is the table?
Where is the blackboard?

LESSON 21

A. Future Tense Negative

Full Form	*Contracted Form*
I will not go.	I won't go.
You will not go.	You won't go.
He will not go.	He won't go.
She will not go.	She won't go.
It will not go.	It won't go.
We will not go.	We won't go.
You will not go.	You won't go.
They will not go.	They won't go.

B. Future Tense Short Answers

Affirmative	*Negative*
Yes, I will.	No, I won't.
Yes, you will.	No, you won't.
Yes, he will.	No, he won't.
Yes, she will.	No, she won't.
Yes, it will.	No, it won't.
Yes, we will.	No, we won't.
Yes, you will.	No, you won't.
Yes, they will.	No, they won't.

II PRACTICE DRILL

Will you be here tomorrow? Yes, I will.
Will you be here on Sunday? No, I won't.
Will we have a new lesson tomorrow? Yes, we will.
Will that team win the game? No, they won't.
Will Cynthia come to class on Tuesday? Yes, she will. No, she won't.
I won't be here tomorrow, will you? Yes, I will.

III EXERCISES

A. Answer these questions using the Future Negative, contracted form.

1. Will you work tomorrow?
   (No, I won't work tomorrow.)

2. Will your friend work tomorrow?
   (No, she won't work tomorrow.)

3. Will you study English tonight?

4. Will he watch television tonight?

5. Will your sister come with you?

6. Will Mr. Flood buy this book?

7. Will Joyce go to the post office?

8. Will she mail her letter?

9. Will they go to Seattle next week?

10. Will Luis eat in the cafeteria?

11. Will the Kowalski family buy that store?

12. Will their son work for them?

13. Will we finish this exercise today?

14. Will the telephone ring?

B. Repeat Exercise A using short affirmative answers.

> **Example: 1. Will you work tomorrow?**
> *(Yes, I will.)*
> 2. Will your friend work tomorrow?
> *(Yes, he will.)*

C. Repeat Exercise A using short negative answers.

> **Example: 1. Will you work tomorrow?**
> *(No, I won't.)*
> 2. Will your friend work tomorrow?
> *(No, she won't.)*

D. Change these sentences to Future Tense, Negative, contracted form.

1. She studies English every day.
(She won't study English every day.)

2. I walk to my office.

3. We write many compositions.

4. They gave me my change.

5. He opened the door for me.

6. The pen will be on the box.

7. Mr. Lazaro lives in New York.

8. I bring my books to class.

9. She waits for us after our lesson.

10. The Rossi family lives near us.

11. Ms. Grant goes to San Francisco.

12. The store will be closed tomorrow.

IV CONVERSATION

Answer these questions.

1. What color is your desk?
2. What colors are you wearing today? (Your shoes, shirt, etc.)
3. What colors do you like?
4. How many colors are in the color chart on the back of this book?
5. Read these problems and give the answers:

   $2 + 5 =$ _____ $6 + 5 =$ _____

   $8 - 3 =$ _____ $3 - 2 =$ _____

   $6 \times 2 =$ _____ $4 \times 3 =$ _____

6. What month is this?
7. What is the day of the month? Of the week?
8. Read these amounts of money:

   $3.63 $0.05 $101.27

LESSON 22

(Review)

I PRACTICE DRILL

I go to the airport
I stand at the information desk.
I ask the clerk when the next plane for Toronto leaves.
The clerk tells me that one leaves at six p.m.
Then I ask, "How much does a one-way ticket cost?"
The clerk answers, "One hundred sixty-five dollars and twelve cents."
I thank her and leave the airport.

II EXERCISES

A. Change these to Future Tense.

1. Marlon studies English
   (Marlon will study English.)

2. I walk to work.

3. He is a good student.

4. He eats at home.

5. The man comes to work on the bus.

6. She opens the door.

7. He puts the mail on the desk.

8. Susan speaks English well.

9. He tells a story to his son.

10. He goes to Washington every week.

11. I am busy today.

12. The woman pays her fare.

13. Mary addresses a letter.

14. They see a movie.

15. The girl signs her name.

16. He likes sandwiches.

17. Mr. Bailey lives in New York.

18. We are in the cafeteria.

19. They hear music every evening.

20. Ms. Berg rides on a bus.

B. Repeat Exercise A using the Future Negative, contracted form.

> **Example: 1. Marlon studies English**
> *(Marlon won't study English.)*

C. Supply the correct opposite.

big _little_	push _____	last _____	stop _____
tall _____	black _____	big _____	late _____
good _____	many _____	pull _____	down _____
happy _____	before _____	white _____	cold _____
in _____	easy _____	few _____	no _____
yes _____	day _____	after _____	out _____
hot _____	sell _____	difficult _____	sad _____
up _____	start _____	night _____	bad _____
first _____	early _____	buy _____	short _____

D. Give complete answers.

1. What is the opposite of *easy*?
   (The opposite of easy is hard.)

2. What is the opposite of *early*?

3. Is *good* the opposite of *bad*?

4. Is *out* the opposite of *down*?

5. Is *short* the opposite of *first*?

6. What is the opposite of *after*?

E. Give only short answers to these questions. Use only *do, does,* or *did* plus the necessary subject pronoun in your answer.

1. Do you like to study English?
   (Yes, I <u>do</u>.)

2. Did you go to Africa last year?
   (No, I didn't.)

3. Do you read the newspaper every morning?

4. Did you study your lesson last night?

5. Did you have an English lesson yesterday?

6. Do you smoke?

7. Does your friend smoke?

8. Does your friend speak English well?

9. Did you go to the movies last night?

10. Do you like this book?

11. Do you learn many new words every day?

12. Did you learn many new words yesterday?

13. Do you walk to your office every day?

14. Did you walk to your office yesterday?

15. Does your teacher speak Spanish?

16. Do you speak Spanish?

17. Does February come before January?

18. Does Wednesday come after Tuesday?

19. Do you eat lunch in the cafeteria every day?

20. Does your friend eat lunch with you every day?

LESSON 23

this, that, these, those

This indicates something near, while *that* indicates something at a distance. The plural of *this* is *these;* the plural of *that* is *those.*

II PRACTICE DRILL

She goes to the airport.
She stands at the information desk.
She asks the clerk when the next plane for Toronto leaves.
The clerk tells her that one leaves at six p.m.
Then she asks, "How much does a one-way ticket cost?"
The clerk answers, "One hundred sixty-five dollars and twelve cents."
She thanks him and leaves the airport.

III EXERCISES

A. Fill in the blanks with *this* or *these.*

1. I like _____ book better than my last one.
   (I like this book better than my last one.)

2. _____ books are written in English.

3. What shall I do with _____ papers?

4. He says _____ pen is his.

5. _____ pen is his but _____ pencils are not.

6. Give _____ letter to Ryan.

7. _____ exercises are not so difficult.

8. _____ room has many windows.

B. Fill in the blanks with *that* or *those.*

1. I gave John _____ book you gave me.
   (I gave John that book you gave me.)

2. _____ men are my friends.

3. _____ boys are his brothers.

82

4. Give _____ letters on the desk to _____ girl in the next room.

5. Is _____ man your father?

6. _____ watch on the desk is a very good one.

7. Does she live in _____ house near the corner?

8. _____ other houses down the street are very beautiful.

C. Choose from among these prepositions and fill in the blanks (about, at, behind, in, of, on, to, with).

1. She lives _____ that house.
   (She lives _in_ that house.)

2. Do you take sugar _____ your coffee?

3. Give the letter _____ Phil.

4. Please give me a piece _____ apple pie.

5. Where do you go _____ lunch?

6. There are many stores _____ Fifth Avenue.

7. We stand _____ the Information Desk.

8. The train leaves _____ ten a.m.

9. The blackboard is _____ the desk.

10. You see _____ your eyes.

11. He comes _____ school _____ the bus.

12. He sits next _____ me.

13. Helen sits _____ front _____ me.

14. I spoke _____ Mr. Steel _____ that matter yesterday.

D. Read this paragraph aloud.

I go to the airport. I stand at the information desk. I ask the clerk when the next plane for Toronto leaves. The clerk tells me that one leaves at six p.m. Then I ask, "How much does a one-way ticket cost?" The clerk answers, "One hundred sixty-five dollars and twelve cents." I thank her and leave the airport.

Read the paragraph again changing the tense from Present to Past.
(I went to the airport, etc.)

E. Repeat Exercise D using the Past Tense and the pronoun *He.*
(He went to the airport, etc.)

IV CONVERSATION

This is a picture of a house.
This house has many windows.
We see that it also has a large roof and a chimney.
Beside the house there is a large tree.
Near the tree there are some bushes.
Inside the house there are many rooms.
On the first floor there are three rooms: a kitchen, a dining room, and a living room.
On the second floor there are several bedrooms and a bathroom.

Answer these questions.

1. What is this a picture of?

2. Does this house have many windows or few windows?

3. Does it have many doors or few doors?

4. Does it have a large roof or a small one?

5. Does it have a chimney? Where is the chimney?

6. Is there a large tree or a small tree beside the house?

84

7. Are there some bushes near the tree?

8. Where can you see some other bushes in this picture?

9. Are there many rooms or few rooms inside the house?

10. What rooms are there on the first floor of this house?

11. What rooms are there on the second floor?

12. Is there only one bedroom on the second floor or are there several bedrooms?

LESSON 24

I GRAMMAR

Comparatives

This cat is big.   The dog is bigger than the cat.

Positive	Comparative	Positive	Comparative
big	bigger	large	larger
small	smaller	cold	colder
tall	taller	easy	easier
late	later	early	earlier
sweet	sweeter	good	better

II PRACTICE DRILL

Asia is larger than Europe.
Europe is smaller than Asia.
Five o'clock is earlier than seven o'clock.
Eight o'clock is later than six o'clock.
This book is good, but that one is better.
The afternoons are cold, but the nights are colder.

III EXERCISES

A. Complete these sentences by filling in the blanks with a comparative. Follow the example in the first sentence.

1. This room is _____ the other room. (large)
   (This room is <u>larger than</u> the other room.)

2. My sister Karen is _____ my mother. (tall)

3. This exercise is _____ the last one. (easy)

4. This book is _____ our last book. (good)

5. I was _____ Henry for the lesson. (late)

6. These lemons are _____ the others. (large)

7. Oranges are _____ lemons. (sweet)

8. I come to the lesson _____ the other students. (early)

9. My book is _____ your book. (small)

10. The weather today is _____ yesterday. (warm)

11. In spring it is _____ in summer. (cool)

12. This lesson is _____ the last one. (good)

13. These exercises are _____ those in the last lesson. (easy)

B. Fill in the blanks with the appropriate comparative.

1. This lesson is *easy*, but the next one will be _____.
   (This lesson is easy, but the next one will be easier.)

2. I got up *early* this morning, but my brother got up _____.

3. This candy is *sweet* but that one is _____.

4. My notebook is *big* but yours is _____.

5. Your car is *small* but mine is _____.

6. His composition is *good* but hers is _____.

IV CONVERSATION

Answer these questions.

1. Do you like coffee better than tea?

2. Are you taller or shorter than your friend?

3. Is New York larger or smaller than Chicago?

4. Is the subway faster or slower than the bus?

5. Is sugar sweeter than lemons?

6. Is winter warmer or cooler than summer?

7. Is June cooler than January?

8. Do you speak English better than you speak your native language?

9. Is February shorter than March?

10. Is John taller or shorter than Linda?

11. Is this lesson easier or more difficult* than lesson 20?

12. Is a horse slower than an automobile?

13. Is ice colder than water?

14. Is Mary older or younger than Susan?

15. Is an hour longer or shorter than a minute?

16. Who is busier, you or your friend?

17. Which is bigger, New York or Chicago?

18. Which is easier, this lesson or the last one?

V REVIEW

A. Choose the correct word.

1. William (speak, speaks) English.
   (William speaks English.)
2. I (don't, doesn't) like to study French.
3. My sister also (doesn't, don't) like to study French.
4. We (don't, doesn't) know how to speak German.
5. Christopher (don't, doesn't) come to the lesson on time.
6. Margo (know, knows) how to play tennis well.
7. We (begin, begins) our lesson on time.
8. (Do, Does) Susannah study with you?
9. (Do, Does) the students in your class speak English well?
10. He (study, studies) English every day.

B. Fill in the blanks.

The days of the week are: _____ _____

_____ _____

_____ _____

_____

---

* With adjectives of more than two syllables we form the comparative by the use of *more,* since to add *-er* to such adjectives would make them difficult to pronounce *(interesting, more interesting; difficult, more difficult).*

The months of the year are:

_____ _____ _____ _____

_____ _____ _____ _____

_____ _____ _____ _____

The four seasons are:

_____ _____ _____ _____

C. Give the word for the numbers from 10 through 25.

_____ _____ _____ _____

_____ _____ _____ _____

_____ _____ _____ _____

_____ _____ _____ _____

LESSON 25

Past Tense

Present	Past		Present	Past
play	played		leave	left
thank	thanked		cost	cost
arrive	arrived		begin	began
carry	carried		know	knew

II EXERCISES

A. Change these sentences to Past Tense.

1. The lesson begins at eight o'clock.
   (The lesson began at eight o'clock.)

2. Howard knows Ms. Angelo.
   (Howard knew Ms. Angelo.)

3. The little girl plays the piano very well.

4. The train leaves at ten o'clock.

5. This dress costs ten dollars.

6. I thank the clerk for the information.

7. The plane arrives in Chicago at nine o'clock.

8. His lunch costs two dollars.

9. Ms. Ryan gives her friend a present.

10. The girl buys a new dress.

11. Mr. Phillips carries a suitcase.

12. I stand in line at the cafeteria.

13. The clerk sells shoes in the store.

14. I buy a suit every year.

15. He always thanks me for my help.

16. The teacher gives us homework.

B. Repeat Exercise A changing the sentences to Past Tense Negative. Use the contracted form.

> **Example: 1.   The lesson begins at eight o'clock.**
> *(The lesson <u>didn't begin</u> at eight o'clock.)*
> **2.   Howard knows Ms. Angelo.**
> *(Howard <u>didn't know</u> Ms. Angelo.)*

C. Repeat Exercise A changing the sentences to Past Tense Questions.

> **Example: 1.   The lesson begins at eight o'clock.**
> *(<u>Did</u> the lesson <u>begin</u> at eight o'clock?)*
> **2.   Howard knows Ms. Angelo.**
> *(<u>Did</u> Howard <u>know</u> Ms. Angelo?)*

D. Change these sentences to Future Tense. Use contractions where possible.

1. Greg speaks English well.
    (Greg <u>will speak</u> English well.)

2. We hear music on the radio.
    (<u>We'll hear</u> music on the radio.)

3. That man and woman have a lot of money.

4. Miss Jacobs knows French well.

5. We are tired today.

6. Terry plays the violin.

7. December is a cold month.

8. The boys eat their food.

9. He stands at the blackboard.

10. We carry small packages.

11. She is a good student.

12. There is no one to help me.

E. Repeat Exercise D changing the sentences to Future Tense Negative. Use the contracted form.

> **Example: 1. Greg speaks English well.**
> *(Greg won't speak English well.)*
> **2.** We hear music on the radio.
> *(We won't hear music on the radio.)*

F. Repeat Exercise D changing the sentences to Future Tense Questions.

> **Example: 1. Greg speaks English well.**
> *(Will Greg speak English well?)*
> **2.** We hear music on the radio.
> *(Will we hear music on the radio?)*

III REVIEW

Add each time word to each sentence. Make any other necessary changes.

1. John rides the bus.
   a) now   *(John is riding the bus now.)*
   b) yesterday   *(John rode the bus yesterday.)*
   c) next week   *(John will ride the bus next week.)*
   d) every day   *(John rides the bus every day.)*

2. Henry goes to English class.
   a) now
   b) yesterday
   c) every day
   d) tomorrow

3. Sally writes in her notebook.
   a) tomorrow
   b) now
   c) every day
   d) last week

4. Mr. and Mrs. James go to Washington.
   a) next Monday
   b) last week
   c) now
   d) every week

5. Sheila takes her books with her.
   a) tomorrow

b) every day
c) now
d) yesterday

6. Miss Barksdale drinks coffee.
   a) now
   b) after breakfast
   c) every afternoon
   d) tomorrow morning

7. He sits in his chair.
   a) tomorrow morning
   b) tonight
   c) yesterday
   d) now

8. They tell good stories.
   a) yesterday
   b) now
   c) every day
   d) tomorrow

9. He put his hat on the table.
   a) now
   b) last night
   c) tomorrow
   d) every afternoon

10. Jim plays the violin.
    a) next week
    b) now
    c) yesterday
    d) every day

IV CONVERSATION

General Questions

Answer these questions.

1. What is your name?

2. How do you spell your name?

3. Do you have a telephone?

4. What is your telephone number?

5. What time is it?

6. What is today's date?

7. What languages do you speak?

8. Where do you work?

9. What is the address of your office?

10. In what department do you work?

11. Are there many or few students in your group?

12. How many times a week do you study?

13. Do you study in the morning or in the evening?

14. On what days of the week do you study English?

15. When did you take your last lesson?

16. When will you take your next lesson?

17. What is the opposite of these words: *small, new, tall, white?*

18. Where do you live?

19. How much is three plus six? Nine plus nine?

20. How much is ten minus five? Ten times five?

LESSON 26

(Review)

I REVIEW

Present Tense *to be*

Affirmative	*Contraction*	*Negative*	*Contraction*	
I am	I'm	I am not	I'm not	
you are	you're	you are not	you're not	you aren't
he is	he's	he is not	he's not	he isn't
she is	she's	she is not	she's not	she isn't
it is	it's	it is not	it's not	it isn't
we are	we're	we are not	we're not	we aren't
you are	you're	you are not	you're not	you aren't
they are	they're	they are not	they're not	they aren't

II EXERCISES

A. Substitute the words in the sentence "I am happy."

> **Example: I am happy.**
> *He*
> He is happy.
> *busy*
> He is busy.

1. He	6. She	11. they're
2. busy	7. Clarence	12. here
3. You	8. We're	13. it isn't
4. late	9. not	14. happy
5. sick	10. Jo	15. I

B. Fill in the blanks.

1. I ＿＿＿＿＿＿ very busy today.
   (I __am__ very busy today.)

2. Lolita ＿＿＿＿＿＿ a good worker.

3. Mr. and Mrs. Angelo ＿＿＿＿＿＿ in Boston.

4. We ＿＿＿＿＿＿ busy this morning.

5. It ＿＿＿＿＿＿ a hot day.

6. Andy ＿＿＿＿＿＿ a good student.

7. He and Eda _____ in the cafeteria.

8. You _____ late for the lesson.

9. They _____ on the first floor.

10. The letters _____ on the desk.

11. He _____ an engineer.

12. They _____ also engineers.

13. We _____ late for work.

14. Helen _____ happy in her work.

15. There _____ someone at the door.

C. Answer these questions using short negative answers.

1. Are you studying Chinese?
   (No, I'm not.)

2. Is your sister studying Russian?
   (No, she isn't. or *No, she's not.)*

3. Are you a bad student?

4. Are Alan and Rudy in school today?

5. Are we in a bus?

6. Is your name Frank?

7. Is the teacher's name Florence?

8. Are the Chalmers' children in the cafeteria?

9. Is today Saturday?

10. Is the door closed?

11. Is your teacher a bad teacher?

12. Are we in the cafeteria?

D. Repeat Exercise C using short affirmative answers.

> **Example: 1. Are you studying Chinese?**
> *(Yes, I am.)*
> **2. Is your sister studying Russian?**
> *(Yes, she is.)*

III REVIEW

Past Tense *to be*

Affirmative	*Negative*	*Contraction*
I was	I was not	I wasn't
you were	you were not	you weren't
he was	he was not	he wasn't
she was	she was not	she wasn't
it was	it was not	it wasn't
we were	we were not	we weren't
you were	you were not	you weren't
they were	they were not	they weren't

IV EXERCISES

A. Substitute the words in the sentence "The teacher was tired."

> **Example: The teacher was tired.**
> *He*
> He was tired.
> *late*
> He was late.

1. He	6. They	11. She
2. late	7. Clara	12. here
3. You	8. We weren't	13. It wasn't
4. busy	9. I was	14. happy
5. not sick	10. not	15. Stan

B. Fill in the blanks.

1. I _____ very tired yesterday.
   (I was very tired yesterday.)

2. Jim _____ in Washington last week.

3. He and his wife _____ here yesterday.

4. We _____ at the movies last night.

5. The books _____ on the desk yesterday.

6. It _____ a hot day yesterday.

7. You _____ not at the lesson last night.

8. I _____ very busy last month.

9. The men _____ hungry and thirsty.

10. Mr. Williams _____ in Florida last winter.

11. He _____ sick yesterday.

12. We _____ late for work yesterday.

13. Helen _____ in the cafeteria at noon.

14. There _____ no one at home when I called.

15. Mr. Everett _____ not at work last week.

C. Change the following sentences to the Past Tense.

1. I am busy today.
   (I _was_ busy _yesterday_.)

2. We are tired today.

3. Jack is in Washington today.

4. He is busy tonight.

5. It is cold today.

6. We are busy this week.

7. They are in Boston today.

8. You are very tired tonight.

9. The books are on my desk today.

10. The weather is good today.

11. Mary is sick today.

12. John and Henry are in Chicago today.

13. There are several students absent today.

14. Mr. Everett is out of town today.

D. Repeat Exercise C using the Past Negative. Use the contracted form wherever possible.

> **Example: 1. I am busy today.**
> (I _wasn't_ busy _yesterday_.)

V CONVERSATION

Is this a hat or a coat?
This is a hat. It's a hat.
Is it a shirt?
No, it isn't. It's not a shirt.

Is this a glass or a cup?
Is it a dish?
What is it?

Are these doors or windows?
Are they chairs?
What are they?

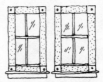

The teacher will ask questions similar to the above about the following objects:

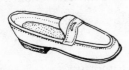

shoe

sweater

shirt

flowers

chairs (2)

watch

LESSON 27

(Review)

I REVIEW

Future Tense *to be*

Affirmative	Contraction	Negative	Contraction
I will be	I'll be	I will not be	I won't be
you will be	you'll be	you will not be	you won't be
he will be	he'll be	he will not be	he won't be
she will be	she'll be	she will not be	she won't be
it will be	it'll be	it will not be	it won't be
we will be	we'll be	we will not be	we won't be
you will be	you'll be	you will not be	you won't be
they will be	they'll be	they will not be	they won't be

II EXERCISES

A. Fill in the blanks.

1. Donald _____ here tomorrow.
   (Donald will be here tomorrow.)

2. Fred and Ethel _____ late for the lesson.

3. They _____ in the cafeteria this afternoon.

4. She _____ in New York next week.

5. I _____ busy tomorrow.

6. We _____ at the lesson tomorrow.

7. Ms. Spencer _____ my teacher next year.

8. It _____ warmer tomorrow.

9. David _____ ten years old tomorrow.

10. Tomorrow _____ Thursday.

B. Change these sentences to Future Tense using contractions wherever possible.

1. He is busy today.
   (He'll be busy tomorrow.)

2. They are late today.

3. He is in Washington this week.

4. Bill and Janice are busy today.

5. Today is Wednesday.

6. We are very busy today.

7. The weather is warm today.

8. Thursday is a holiday.

9. Henry is in Dallas today.

10. The men are at home today.

C. Repeat Exercise B using the Future Tense Negative. Use contractions wherever possible.

> **Example: 1. He is busy today.**
> *(He won't be busy tomorrow.)*

III REVIEW

Future Tense Short Answers

Yes, I will.	No, I won't.	Yes, we will.	No, we won't.
Yes, you will.	No, you won't.	Yes, you will.	No, you won't.
Yes, he will.	No, he won't.		
Yes, she will.	No, she won't.	Yes, they	No, they
Yes, it will.	No, it won't.	will.	won't.

IV EXERCISES

A. Answer these questions using short affirmative answers.

1. Will the telephone ring?
   (Yes, it will.)

2. Will you be here tomorrow?

3. Will we finish this lesson soon?

4. Will Coretta work for them?

5. Will you work tomorrow?

6. Will you come to class next week?

7. Will he watch TV tonight?

8. Will she watch TV with him?

9. Will they go to Mexico City next month?

10. Will your friend eat in the cafeteria?

11. Will the Walesa family buy that store?

12. Will we walk to school tomorrow?

B. Repeat Exercise A using short negative answers.

> **Example: 1. Will the telephone ring?**
> *(No, it won't.)*

V REVIEW

Opposites

> **Example: What's the opposite of *pull*?**
> The opposite of *pull* is *push*.

Following the above example, give the opposite for each of these words.

little _big_	out _____	stop _____
open _____	after _____	new _____
under _____	last _____	before _____
husband _____	find _____	shut _____
down _____	girl _____	soft _____
brother _____	daughter _____	black _____
sell _____	sister _____	night _____
good _____	begin _____	dirty _____
dark _____	late _____	empty _____
summer _____	fast _____	uptown _____
absent _____	woman _____	east _____
wife _____	unhappy _____	easy _____
sit _____	sour _____	boy _____

VI CONVERSATION

What's this? Is it a map?
Is it a notebook? A calendar?

JANUARY								FEBRUARY								MARCH					
S	M	T	W	T	F	S		S	M	T	W	T	F	S		S	M	T	W	T	F	S
						1				1	2	3	4	5				1	2	3	4	5
2	3	4	5	6	7	8		6	7	8	9	10	11	12		6	7	8	9	10	11	12
9	10	11	12	13	14	15		13	14	15	16	17	18	19		13	14	15	16	17	18	19
16	17	18	19	20	21	22		20	21	22	23	24	25	26		20	21	22	23	24	25	26
23	24	25	26	27	28	29		27	28							27	28	29	30	31		
30	31																				

Answer these questions.

1. What is the date today?

2. Is today Tuesday?

3. Is today Wednesday?

4. Was yesterday Saturday?

5. Was yesterday Monday?

6. Will tomorrow be Sunday?

7. How many days are there in a week?

8. What is the first day of the week?

9. What is the last day of the week?

10. Do you work on Monday?

11. Do you work on Sunday?

12. On what days do you work?

13. What month is this?

14. How many months are there in a year?

15. What is the first month of the year?

16. What is the last month of the year?

17. What are the principal holidays in the United States?

18. What are the principal holidays in your native country?

LESSON 28

(Review)

I REVIEW

Tenses—Time Expressions

today	now
tomorrow	next week
yesterday	last week

II EXERCISES

A. Add the time expressions to each sentence making other necessary changes. Use pronouns and contractions wherever possible.

1. Peter is busy.
    a) today   *(He's busy today.)*
    b) tomorrow.   *(He'll be busy tomorrow.)*
    c) yesterday   *(He was busy yesterday.)*

2. There are fifteen people in class.
    a) last week
    b) today
    c) next week

3. We were at a party.
    a) tomorrow night
    b) last night
    c) now

4. Donald is ten years old.
    a) last year
    b) today
    c) next Thursday

5. The weather is cool.
    a) last week
    b) next week
    c) today

6. Ms. Bennett is at the theater.
    a) last night
    b) tonight
    c) this weekend

7. I was late for class.
   a) last night
   b) tomorrow night
   c) now

8. The classroom was not empty.
   a) now
   b) last night
   c) tomorrow night

9. My teacher is happy.
   a) now
   b) yesterday
   c) tomorrow

10. Mr. Taylor is in Dallas.
    a) last week
    b) now
    c) next week

B. Fill in the blanks with the correct form of *to be*.

1. I _____ very busy today.
   (I <u>am</u> very busy today.)

2. We _____ very busy yesterday.

3. Ben _____ in Philadelphia yesterday.

4. We _____ at the movies last night.

5. They _____ in the cafeteria now.

6. The window _____ open all last night.

7. He _____ here at two o'clock tomorrow.

8. John and Donald _____ in Boston last week.

9. We _____ very tired last night.

10. The books _____ on this desk yesterday.

11. The men _____ here at noon tomorrow.

12. I think the weather _____ warm tomorrow.

13. I _____ very cold yesterday.

14. David _____ always late for his lesson.

15. He _____ late yesterday.

16. Mary _____ in the restaurant now.

17. I _____ five minutes late for my lesson last night.

18. I think he _____ very busy tomorrow.

19. We _____ all very busy in our office yesterday.

20. Harry _____ in Washington all next week.

21. My daughter _____ very sick last night.

22. Linda and Judy _____ at our home last night.

C. Repeat Exercise B using contractions wherever possible.

> **Example: 1. I'm very busy today.**

III REVIEW

Personal Pronouns

Subject	Object	Subject	Object
I	me	we	us
you	you	you	you
he	him		
she	her	they	them
it	it		

Substitute the correct personal pronoun for the italicized word or words. Use contractions wherever possible.

1. *Ms. Salazar* is in her office.
   (*She's in her office.*)

2. *The book* is on the desk.

3. *Don and Phil* are in the restaurant.

4. Do you study with *George*?

5. I eat lunch with *Henry and William* every day.

6. *Those books* are very old.

7. *The maid* opened the door for us.

8. He put *his hat* on and went out.

9. He always speaks to *Mary and me* in English.

10. I spoke to *Terry* about it.

11. *Helen and I* want to learn English.

12. I like *George* very much.

IV REVIEW

there is, there are

There is one Monday every week.
There are fifty-two Mondays every year.

Choose the correct word.

1. There (is, are) one telephone in our office.
   (There is one telephone in our office.)

2. There (is, are) seven days in a week.

3. There (is, are) twelve months in a year.

4. There (is, are) a book on the table.

5. There (is, are) some books on the table.

6. There (is, are) several pictures on the wall.

7. There (is, are) a newspaper on the desk.

8. There (is, are) twenty-four hours in a day.

9. There (is, are) many men in that office.

10. There (is, are) two chairs in this room.

V CONVERSATION

A. Answer these questions.

1. Is there a bed in the room?

2. Are there three chairs in the room?

3. Is there a table in the room?

4. Is there a tablecloth on the table?

5. Is there a plant on the table?

6. Are there five pictures on the wall?

7. Are there two windows in this room?

8. Are there window shades on the window?

9. Are there two doors in this room?

10. Is there a rug on the floor?

11. Are there two pillows on the bed?

12. Is there a closet in this room?

B. Answer these questions.

1. How many beds are there in this room?

2. How many chairs are there in this room?

3. How many tables are there in this room?

4. How many windows are there in this room?

5. How many pillows are there on the bed?

6. How many doors are there in the room?

7. How many closets are there in the room?

8. How many rugs are there in the room?

LESSON 29

(Review)

I REVIEW

there

there is	there are
there was	there were

II EXERCISES

A. Change the following sentences to Past Tense.

1. There is a typewriter in the room.
   (There was a typewriter in the room.)

2. There are many people in the room.
   (There were many people in the room.)

3. There are three books on the desk.

4. There is a baby in the room.

5. There is a secretary in his office.

6. There are two children in the room.

7. There are ten men at the meeting.

8. There are two pianos in the apartment.

9. There are many people in the audience.

10. There is a letter here for you.

11. There are three students in our group.

12. There are two chairs at the table.

13. There are many offices in the building.

14. There is a policeman on the corner.

15. There are three telephones in the office.

16. There is a window in the room.

17. There is an automobile at the door.

18. There are two radios in the room.

19. There is a library in the building.

20. There is a cup and saucer on the table.

B. Repeat Exercise A changing the sentences to Future Tense.

> **Example: 1. There is a typewriter in the room.**
> *(There will be a typewriter in the room.)*
> 2. There are many people in the room.
> *(There will be many people in the room.)*

C. Repeat Exercise A changing the sentences to the Negative form.

> **Example: 1. There is a typewriter in the room.**
> *(There isn't a typewriter in the room.)*
> 2. There are many people in the room.
> *(There aren't many people in the room.)*

D. Repeat Exercise A changing the sentences to Question form.

> **Example: 1. There is a typewriter in the room.**
> *(Is there a typewriter in the room?)*
> 2. There are many people in the room.
> *(Are there many people in the room?)*

III REVIEW

Plurals

Write the plural of the following.

address	*addresses*	class	
American	*Americans*	conversation	
answer		corner	
apple		daughter	
arm		day	
avenue		desk	
banana		dinner	
blackboard		door	

body* _____	drink _____
book _____	egg _____
boy _____	eye _____
breakfast _____	father _____
bus _____	finger _____
cafeteria _____	fish _____
chair _____	foot _____
city _____	Friday _____
language _____	Russian _____
leg _____	sandwich _____
lesson _____	Saturday _____
lunch _____	sign _____
man _____	son _____
match _____	street _____
meal _____	Sunday _____
Monday _____	teacher _____
month _____	thumb _____
mother _____	Thursday _____

IV CONVERSATION

A. Answer the following questions giving a short negative answer first followed by the correct answer.

1. Are there thirteen months in a year?
   (No, there aren't. There are twelve months in a year.)

2. Is there a picture on the wall?
   (No, there isn't. There's a calendar on the wall.)

3. Is there a day called Firstday?

4. Is there a month called Maytember?

* Nouns ending in -y, preceded by a consonant, change the -y to i before adding -es (body, *bodies*; city, *cities*, etc.).

5. Is there a clock on your desk?

6. Is there a rug on the window?

7. Are there eight days in a week?

8. Are there fifty minutes in an hour?

9. Are there seventy seconds in a minute?

10. Are there forty days in a month?

11. Are there thirty days in February?

12. Are there thirty-two days in January?

13. Are there four hands on a clock?

14. Are there five seasons in a year?

15. Are there more people in Washington than in New York?

16. Are there two presidents of the United States?

17. Are there fifty-two states in the United States?

18. Are there fifty-four weeks in a year?

19. Are there twenty-eight hours in a day?

B. Describe the room you are studying in. Begin each sentence with *there is* or *there are.*

LESSON 30

(Review)

I REVIEW

Third Person

$$\left.\begin{array}{l} \textbf{he} \\ \textbf{she} \\ \textbf{it} \end{array}\right\} \underline{\hspace{3cm}}\textbf{s}$$

II EXERCISES

A. Choose the correct word

   1. Stephanie (go, goes) to her lesson every day.
       (Stephanie goes to her lesson every day.)
   2. They (go, goes) to work early.
   3. He (live, lives) in New York.
   4. We (like, likes) our apartment.
   5. This motor (work, works) well.
   6. The time (go, goes) quickly.
   7. You (speak, speaks) well.
   8. Ethel also (speak, speaks) well.
   9. He (come, comes) here every day.
   10. They (go, goes) to bed very late.
   11. He (go, goes) to bed very late.
   12. William and Mary both (study, studies) hard.

B. Change *I* to *she* or *he* in the following sentences.

   1. I work hard every day.
       (She works hard every day. or *He works hard every day.)*

   2. I study every evening.

   3. I go to the office every morning.

   4. I ride the bus to work.

   5. I like Miami.

   6. I go to the movies every Saturday.

   7. I live in Texas.

   8. I have two brothers.

9. I want to learn English.

10. I am happy.

C. Repeat Exercise B changing *I* to *My teacher.*

1. I work hard every day.
(My teacher works hard every day.)

III REVIEW

Tenses and Personal Pronouns

A. Read this paragraph aloud.

Every morning William gets up at seven o'clock. He washes and dresses. Then he has his breakfast. He leaves his home about eight o'clock. He takes the bus to work. He arrives at his office about nine o'clock. He works until noon. At noon he goes to the cafeteria and has his lunch. Then he returns to his office and works until six o'clock. At six o'clock he goes to his home. He eats his dinner about seven o'clock. At eleven o'clock he goes to bed.

B. Read the paragraph again changing *William* and *he* to *we* and *his* to *our.*

(Every morning we get up at seven o'clock.)

C. Read the paragraph again changing *William* and *he* to *I* and *his* to *my.*

(Every morning I get up at seven o'clock.)

D. Read the paragraph again changing all the verbs to Past Tense. Add any words you need in order to make this tense change.

(<u>Yesterday</u> William <u>got up</u> at seven o'clock.)

E. Answer these questions. Listen to the time used in the questions and be careful to answer the question in the same time.

1. What does William do at seven o'clock in the morning?

2. What is he going to do at eleven o'clock at night?

3. What is he doing at noon?

4. When does he arrive at his office?

5. When is he going home?

6. What is he going to do after he gets home?

7. What does he do after lunch?

8. What did he do before breakfast?

9. When is he going to go to bed?

10. When will he get up?

11. When is he going to return to his office?

12. How does he go to work?

13. Where will he eat lunch?

14. What does he do between eight o'clock and nine o'clock?

IV CONVERSATION

wood	rubber	leather
glass	paper	stone
metal	cloth	plastic
steel	copper	cotton
iron	wool	silk

Answer these questions.

1. What is a table made of?
   (A table is made of wood.)

2. What is a pencil made of?

3. What is a pen made of?

4. What is a window made of?

5. What are shoes made of?

6. What is a suit made of?

7. What is a dress made of?

8. What is a lamp made of?

9. What is a pillow made of?

10. What is a briefcase made of?

11. What are keys made of?

12. What are curtains made of?

13. What is a knife made of?

14. What is a notebook made of?

15. What is a hat made of?

16. What are erasers made of?

17. What are bricks made of?

18. What is a mirror made of?

LESSON 31

(Review)

I REVIEW

Possessive Adjectives

I	my		we	our
you	your		you	your
he	his			
she	her		they	their
it	its			

He knows *his* lesson well.
They know *their* lessons well.

II EXERCISE

Fill in the blank with the possessive adjective corresponding to the subject of the sentence.

1. I like _____ teacher very much.
   (I like my teacher very much.)

2. John also likes _____ teacher.

3. The men are in _____ office.

4. She studies _____ lesson.

5. Mr. Santos reads _____ newspaper.

6. Charles and Ellen prepare _____ lessons.

7. A good student studies _____ lessons every day.

8. He likes _____ new car.

9. I eat _____ lunch in the cafeteria.

10. You have on _____ new suit today.

11. Mr. and Mrs. Street will soon move to _____ new apartment.

12. John is on _____ vacation.

13. Mary will go on _____ vacation next week.

14. The President meets _____ Cabinet today.

15. We have all _____ meals at home.

16. Charles and Diana have _____ dinner at the same time.

17. We like _____ new apartment.

18. He likes _____ teacher.

19. She prepares _____ lessons well.

20. They do _____ work well.

21. Ms. Tyrone teaches _____ class in this room.

III REVIEW

Telling Time

A. What time is it?

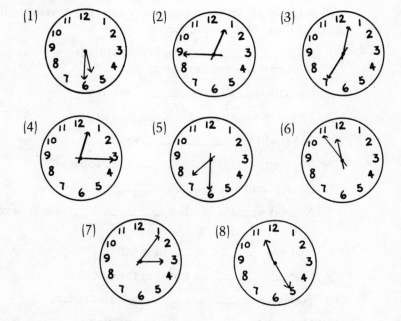

(1) (2) (3)

(4) (5) (6)

(7) (8)

B. Answer these questions.

1. What time do you get up every morning?

2. What time do you have breakfast?

3. What time do you have lunch?

4. What time do you have dinner?

5. What time does your lesson begin?

6. What time does your lesson end?

7. What time do you begin your work?

8. What time do you finish your work?

9. What time is it now?

10. What time do you go to bed?

11. How long does your lesson last?

12. How many hours do you work every day?

13. How many hours do you sleep every night?

14. How long do you study English every day?

15. How long do you study every day?

IV REVIEW

Short Answers

Answer these questions using short answers only. Be sure to use the correct tense.

1. Did she come to class yesterday?
   (Yes, she did. or *No, she didn't.)*

2. Is his name Ivan?
   (No, it isn't. or *Yes, it is.)*

3. Will you eat lunch with me?
   (Yes, I will. or *No, I won't.)*

4. Do you smoke?

5. Did your friend like the movie last night?

6. Is your father studying English?

7. Will your parents be home today?

8. Will we finish this exercise today?

9. Am I speaking very fast?

10. Are the Timberlakes in class today?

11. Will they be in class tomorrow?

12. Were they in class yesterday?

13. Do you like this book?

14. Did your sister study Chinese last year?

15. Is today Wednesday?

16. Am I tall?

17. Did you finish your lesson last night?

18. Will your brother eat in the cafeteria?

19. Are we almost finished with this book?

20. Do you speak Spanish?

21. Are you short?

V CONVERSATION

Use the color chart on the back of this book to ask questions about colors.

> **Example: 1. (Pointing) What's this color?**
> *(It's brown.)*
> 2. What color is this book?
> *(It's blue.)*
> 3. What color is my shirt?
> 4. What color is the wall?